TQM: 50 WAYS TO MAKE IT WO[illegible] J

JoAnn B. Haberer
MaryLou Wendel Webb

A FIFTY-MINUTE™ SERIES BOOK

CRISP PUBLICATIONS, INC.
Menlo Park, California

TQM: 50 WAYS TO MAKE IT WORK FOR YOU

JoAnn B. Haberer

MaryLou Wendel Webb

CREDITS:
Editor: **Sara Schneider**
Layout and Composition: **Interface Studio**
Cover Design: **Carol Harris**
Artwork: **Ralph Mapson**

English language Crisp books are distributed worldwide. Our major international distributors include:

CANADA: Reid Publishing, Ltd., Box 69559—109 Thomas St., Oakville, Ontario Canada L6J 7R4. TEL: (416) 842-4428, FAX: (416) 842-9327

AUSTRALIA: Career Builders, P. O. Box 1051, Springwood, Brisbane, Queensland, Australia 4127. TEL: 841-1061, FAX: 841-1580

NEW ZEALAND: Career Builders, P. O. Box 571, Manurewa, Auckland, New Zealand. TEL: 266-5276, FAX: 266-4152

JAPAN: Phoenix Associates Co., Mizuho Bldg. 2-12-2, Kami Osaki, Shinagawa-Ku, Tokyo 141, Japan. TEL: 3-443-7231, FAX: 3-443-7640

Selected Crisp titles are also available in other languages. Contact International Rights Manager Suzanne Kelly at (415) 323-6100 for more information.

Library of Congress Catalog Card Number 93-73149
Haberer, JoAnn B. and MaryLou Wendel Webb
ISBN 1-56052-256-9

This book is printed on recyclable paper with soy ink.

ABOUT THIS BOOK

TQM: 50 Ways to Make It Work for You is not like most books. It stands out in an important way. It is not a book to read—it is a book to *use*. The "self-paced" format and many worksheets encourage readers to get involved and try new ideas immediately.

We hope that this book will help you understand what Total Quality Management is and how it can work for you. But perhaps equally important, we hope that you will use it to renew vitality in your job and your organization. After all, our jobs aren't just about global competitiveness and market share; there should be some *living* in the term "working for a living."

TQM: 50 Ways to Make It Work for You (and other titles listed in the back of this book) can be used effectively a number of ways. Here are some possibilities:

- **Individual Study.** Because the book is self-instructional, all that is needed is a quiet place, committed time, and a pencil. By completing the activities and exercises, you receive both valuable feedback and action steps for improving the effectiveness of your company.
- **Workshops and Seminars.** This book was developed from hundreds of interactive seminars and contains many exercises that work well with group participation. The book is also a refresher for future reference by workshop attendees.
- **Remote Location Training.** This book is an excellent self-study resource for managers, supervisors, and managerial candidates not able to attend "home office" training sessions.

Even after this book has been used for training and applied in real situations, it will remain a valuable source of ideas for reflection.

ABOUT THE AUTHORS

JoAnn B. Haberer is the CEO and a co-owner of Action Training Systems, Inc., a company that designs and produces training programs. She has been an instructional designer and writer for all types of adult-learning audiences, including welfare-to-work programs, technical training for engineers, and management-level skill-enhancement programs.

Ms. Haberer has a B.A. in Education from the University of Washington and an M.A. in Educational Psychology from the University of Colorado. She has taught graduate-level Employee Relations classes at Chapman College in Orange, California, and management seminars in Employee Coaching and Counseling for Portland Community College in Oregon.

Ms. Haberer has published a number of articles on Total Quality Management principles in the workplace.

MaryLou Wendel Webb has been involved in the development of people, programs, and resources since 1973. She has managed her own business, Quality Improvement Strategies. Her clients include Tektronix, Intel, the National Management Association, Good Samaritan Hospital, the Portland Chamber of Commerce, and the State of Oregon.

Ms. Webb is currently Dean of the Management and Professional Development Division for Portland Community College. She is responsible for the design, marketing, coordination, sales of management and professional development training programs.

Ms. Webb holds a B.A. and an M.A. in Education from Portland State University in Oregon. She served as Director of Alumni Affairs for Portland State University, and has been a member of the Advisory Board for *Oregon Business Magazine,* which has published her articles on Total Quality Management, Customer Service, and Team Building. She is an active participant in hearings for the State of Oregon Legislative Committee on Trade and Economic Development and the Oregon Quality Initiative.

PREFACE

Will It Work for You?

Total Quality Management has been declared to be both "the cavalry coming to the rescue" and "the last nail in the coffin" of American business in the 1990s. What will it do at *your* company or organization? Will it succeed—or fail? Will it be worth all the effort and money to design and implement new systems and paperwork, or will it drain already low resources?

If you are skeptical about TQM—skeptical about what it will do to your organization, to your work style, to *you*—this book is for you. Its goal is to give you concepts you can *use*—as a member of your company or organization, as a member of a team, and as an individual.

TQM challenges organizations and individuals to look at the *way* things are done as well as *what* is done. And, once it becomes a natural part of your job, we believe you will agree that the change and uncertainty was worth it.

JoAnn B Haberer MaryLou Wendel Webb

JoAnn Haberer MaryLou Webb

DEDICATION

To my husband, Tom, who has raised ''active listening''
to an art form.
JBH

To my children, Crayton and Tenley, who have been
my focus for continuous improvement.
MWW

CONTENTS

INTRODUCTION

If you have looked over any literature on Total Quality Management (TQM), you may have found, as we did, that understanding and implementing TQM appear to be either very complex or almost foolishly simple. We believe, however, that the real "meaning" of TQM lies somewhere in the middle. It isn't *that* difficult—and it isn't just a new bunch of silly acronyms and buzzwords either.

This book distills the basic philosophy of TQM to 50 straightforward, effective ideas for learning and implementing TQM concepts.

We encourage you to use the information in this book as a *starting point* for your own unique ideas. We realize that some of the 50 suggestions may not be directly applicable to your department or organization. Try to "tweak" these into a form that *will* work for you. That will be a good start in actually applying TQM in your workplace. TQM depends on creative "tweaking" to make things better.

One way this book can work for you is to provide your team with "grist for the mill." Each week pick one of its ideas to use as a discussion starter at your team meeting. Team meetings are meant to be both problem-solving sessions and *process* opportunities. If you use your team meetings *only* to define and solve problems, they will become tedious after a few months. We believe that if you use part of your team meeting time to discuss the *process* of what you are doing, trying to continuously improve on that process, your meetings will be more enjoyable and productive.

Total Quality Management (TQM) programs—under a variety of names—have been both wild successes and miserable failures at different organizations. How can this be? How can a good idea work wonders in one organization and not be at all workable in another? Perhaps the reason lies in the fact that TQM is just that, an *idea*, not a packaged system or an off-the-shelf program.

The organizations for which TQM is rewarding understands and applies *all* of the basic concepts of Total Quality Management—not just those it happens to immediately agree with or those that would be easy to implement. The *form* that TQM takes will vary from organization to organization, but the *concepts* are always the same.

TQM can be summed up as an all-encompassing process that involves everyone in the organization in identifying and improving every aspect of service and every product. Seems like a lot to ask of people, doesn't it? Well, it is.

A basic TQM concept is that you must rely on *facts* rather than intuition to make decisions. Management has long prided itself on its ability to make decisions based on "gut feelings." But TQM requires management to get the facts before decisions are made. From product development to marketing to customer service—TQM organizations use facts based on information they have sought out from various sources, including customers, competitors' products, and their own employees.

All successful Total Quality Management programs have one principle in common: They measure and keep on measuring. Each measurement provides factual feedback for the next round of improvements. TQM embraces the adage "what gets measured gets improved."

TQM Is Effective, but Not Necessarily Easy

Quality requires a total commitment from all levels of the organization—from top management support to full employee involvement. This is not easy. Some organizations retreat from TQM after a short-term program, saying it will not work for them. These organizations have usually not accepted the *total* in Total Quality Management. It is a new way of thinking that requires us to be much more competitive, much more concerned about the little things that make our customers either love us or hate us. But just as the steam engine revolutionized the agricultural society, TQM will revolutionize the information society.

As long as we have facts available, we cannot afford to not use them. Your competition, whether it is domestic or international, has the same set of facts.

Once the facts are available, they are used to make both physical and mental changes to the workplace. TQM organizations make changes based on the following objectives:

- **Focus on the customer**
- **Involve the entire workforce in decision-making**
- **Commit to continuous improvement**

These three objectives form the basis of the entire TQM effort. By understanding these objectives, and how they can be *specifically applied* to your organization, you will have captured the essence of Total Quality Management.

Focus on the Customer
Achieving quality means matching (or exceeding) your customer's expectations with the performance of your product or service. A focus on the customer shifts an organization's emphasis from narrow internal problems to the much larger marketplace—"how will this affect our customers?"

Involve the Entire Workforce in Decision-Making
TQM organizations don't just tolerate the input and ideas of their employees, they *rely* on them. The usual decision-making and action-generating unit is not an individual manager but rather a team of employees.

A team relies on cooperative effort to achieve a goal that no individual could accomplish. Teams use cooperation and consensus to get the job done, but this does not mean that team members must always agree or must always be passive. Some of the best ideas and most innovative solutions come from heated discussions and passionate disagreements.

Commit to Continuous Improvement
Continuous improvement simply means never resting on your laurels. Regardless of the product or service, it can always be improved. Even the "perfect" product becomes outdated, or isn't appropriate for everyone. How can you refine it just a bit more—make it more "user friendly," or perhaps make the packaging more environmentally sound?

The nemesis of continuous improvement is "good enough." This car is "good enough," this package delivery schedule is "good enough," this brain surgery is "good enough." What may be "good enough" today will be outdated, unusable, and old-fashioned very soon. The TQM organization does not wait for the day that their product or service is eclipsed by the competition. They are working *today* on improvements that will be implemented long before their customers become dissatisfied.

Action Plans

Action Plans are contracts that state what will be done, by whom and by what date and time. Action Plans are important because by writing down this information you can be sure that everyone has heard the same message. One of the leading causes of *lack of progress* is *lack of communication*—"Oh, I didn't know you wanted *me* to do that!" or "You mean that was supposed to be finished *today*?"

Action Plans should be used whenever you have something to make, something to check on, something to bring, something to find, something to get approved, something to ask, something to *do.*

Action Plans should be part of the meeting minutes, or they can be used in lieu of the minutes, because they tell the story of what was discussed and what decisions were made. Everyone should have easy access to the Action Plans.

Of course, the Action Plan is the place to begin your next meeting. Did everyone meet his or her goal and deadline? If not, what problems kept each team member from achieving these goals, and what Action Plans can be made to overcome the problems?

Once you and your team start using Action Plans, you will wonder how you ever survived without them. They save time and paperwork, and more importantly, they maintain good communication and good working relationships among team members.

ACTION PLAN

Objective:

Task:	Person(s) Responsible	Deadline Date
1. ________		
2. ________		
3. ________		

Follow-Up Conducted? ________

SECTION

1

Take Personal Responsibility for Quality

Make a Commitment to Never-Ending Improvement

Dr. Edwards Deming, author of *Out of the Crisis*, and the "father" of the TQM movement approaches quality as a quest for continuous improvement. This should become the way an organization does business. Perhaps part of the reason the United States lost its edge in world markets is that it became satisfied with its status quo. The United States saw itself at the height of its capabilities, with no room for improvement.

Excellence—Whether in a National Endeavor, a Company, an Athletic Competition, or a Personal Goal—Comes from the Never-Ending Pursuit of Improvement.

Consider some of the ways that continuous improvement has affected our lives: In the 1950s polio was killing and crippling thousands of children each year. What would have happened if medical researchers had tried one possible cure, found it didn't work and just gave up? Or consider the "man on the moon" program. If the NASA engineers had been content with just "good enough" calculations, what are the odds that the astronauts would have actually arrived on the moon? And if the U.S. wasn't willing to do the work, and re-do it until it was perfect, might another country such as the former U.S.S.R. have been willing?

It may be hard to see your work in such a significant or competitive spirit, but global markets today make continuous improvement mandatory. Other countries scoff at American companies who sat back in the 1970s and 1980s and allowed their markets to be taken by competitors who were willing to do the same job a little better, a little more efficiently, and with a lot more attention to the customer.

Dr. Deming contends that "there is no such thing as getting it right with quality." Whenever you reach a point of satisfaction with your product or service, it is time to push on to the next improvement.

COMMITMENT TO QUALITY CHECK

When was the last time you improved your product or service? ______________________

What is the next improvement that you believe *should* be made? ______________________

What prevents you from making that improvement *right now*? ______________________

TIP 2

Honor Your Commitments

The way you handle the commitments you make says a lot about your priorities. The old adage "Power is defined by who keeps whom waiting" is based on the fact that a person who is late for an appointment assumes he or she is more important than the person who is waiting. Why else show up 10 minutes beyond the set time? Latecomers assume that whatever they were doing that caused them to be late is more important than whatever it was the other people were doing when they stopped to go to the appointment.

If you are often late for appointments, think about why. Most people who are chronically late blame it on circumstances—"The traffic was *horrible*," or "I got stuck on the phone with that guy from purchasing again"—but the fact is they are late because being on time is not a priority for them.

There are two kinds of commitments: *clear* commitments and *vague* commitments. Clear commitments are verbal or written promises that both sides understand and agree to keep, such as employment contracts, government laws and marriage vows.

Vague commitments are those cultural and organizational commitments that you are expected to "just know" and obey. For example, there is certain behavior expected of employees toward their supervisors, of men toward women (and vice versa), and of children at adult social functions.

Many people have trouble keeping vague commitments. In many instances these expected standards are not in line with their personal values. In some societies, people might have the freedom to not keep vague commitments (but they still must suffer the societal consequences).

Clear commitments are another story. It is imperative that you *know* and *keep* the clearly defined commitments that you make to your organization and to your team members. If you can't make a commitment in good faith, it is better not to make it in the first place rather than to break it later.

Consider your clear commitments. Do you do what you commit to because you value the time and effort of others on your team? Or do you have personal agendas that keep you constantly apologizing for not showing up on time or not having your part of the project finished?

CHECK YOUR COMMITMENTS

If you have problems keeping your clearly defined agreements, what can you do to change that? ______________________

____

____

____

What about others on your team? List clear commitments that are often broken by one or more members. ______________________

____

____

____

Use this three-step process to help ensure understanding and cooperation in meeting commitments.

1. Make all commitments *clear*—write them down.

2. Ask every team member to agree personally to the commitment; sign off each one.

3. Follow up on a broken commitment by acknowledging it and asking the person responsible to find a way to avoid it happening again, and present that option to the team. (Notice that this is not a blame-placing activity; the focus is on solving the problem.)

TIP 3

Make a Daily "To Do" List

It is important to discipline yourself to keep on target each day. Many of us make a list when we get overwhelmed, but do not bother to do it when we are dealing with just everyday matters.

A daily "To Do" list helps you see how you spend your time, whether or not you are accomplishing your goals. Time is the one thing we never seem to have enough of, and it must be managed well to use it wisely.

In an atmosphere of continuous improvement, the "To Do" list is a snapshot of your short- and long-term tasks and goals. You may want to keep your daily lists in a small notebook or calendar so you can go back and see how much you have accomplished over a given period of time. This gives you confidence that you are making progress and that improvement has been a continuing process for you.

Can you see how a daily list might help you become more organized and efficient?

In your work situation what kind of things would be on your daily "To Do" list?

- ______________________________
- ______________________________
- ______________________________
- ______________________________
- ______________________________

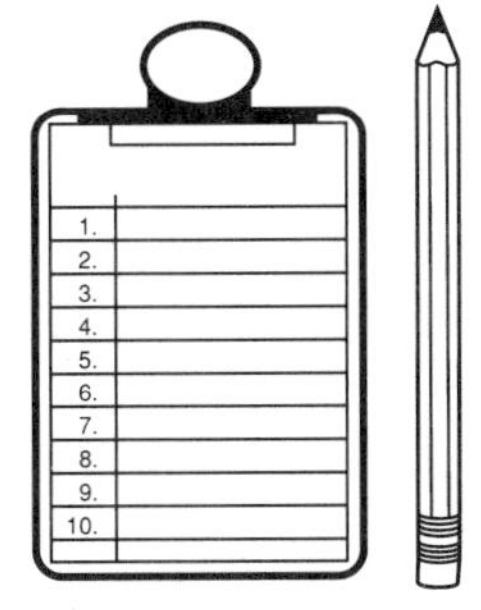

Using the following example, design a "To Do List" that you can copy and use to keep yourself on target.

(Sample)

TO DO LIST

Date: ______________________________

Priority Task Completed/Status

( ) ____

( ) ____

( ) ____

( ) ____

( ) ____

( ) ____

( ) ____

( ) ____

( ) ____

( ) ____

( ) ____

Can you see how a list of weekly "To Dos" for your team might be a helpful extension of this process?

TIP 4

Accept Help Graciously

Sometimes it is difficult to accept help from others because you think it makes you look ineffective or weak. In TQM organizations, offering and accepting help when it is needed is a part of the teamwork culture.

Not accepting help and then blowing a deadline or having to make excuses for not finishing an Action Plan assignment carries a much greater stigma than accepting assistance.

Asking for help is not an admission of failure; it is an affirmation that you value the commitment you have made to your team and your organization. You want to see that the goal is reached, the deadline is met, the work is delivered as promised. As a team member you can feel free to ask for help and know that later you will be asked to help in return.

If you find yourself *constantly* seeking the help of others to meet your assignments and deadlines, talk with your supervisor or other team members about how you might improve your productivity or organize your work load.

Check any of the following that apply:

☐ Are you taking on too much?

☐ Is your estimation process overly optimistic?

☐ Do you need some help with time management?

Again, asking for help is your first step in overcoming inefficiency.

HOW WELL DO YOU ACCEPT HELP?

Think about times when you wanted to ask for help but were concerned about how it would look to others.

When did you ask for assistance and it was refused? ______________________________

Why did that happen? ______________________________

Discuss in your team the process for assigning the work load and asking for help when it is needed. ______________________________

TIP 5

Lead When a Leader Is Needed

Is it confusing to hear that you will be part of a team, that consensus will be the method of deciding things, and then that "leadership" is a high priority in Total Quality Management? Why are leaders needed when everyone in the team has an equal voice and all decisions will be made as a group? The answer lies in the definition of the word "leader." A leader by TQM standards is one who "guides the group." This does not mean "runs the group" or "dictates to the group."

A leader could be a member of the group who has personal experience or technical expertise in an area that the group is working on. For example, suppose your team has decided to publish a bimonthly newsletter to communicate what is going on in your department to the other members of your company. One of your team members is proficient in desktop publishing and assumes a *leadership role* in getting the newsletter ready for printing. Other team members will have ideas and will help get the newsletter ready, but the person who has the expertise will "guide" the group through the decisions that will need to be made about the layout and then will probably be responsible for seeing that it is done correctly.

ARE YOU WILLING TO LEAD?

Think of the expertise or experience that you bring to your team. Write down one or two areas or situations in which you feel you could lead.

____

____

____

How does your team select people to assume a leadership role on a project?

____

____

____

TIP 6

Define "Excellence" for Yourself

Much of what is intimidating about Total Quality Management is new terms and jargon. "Excellence" is one of those words that seems to have lost its meaning through overuse. What does it really mean to achieve "excellence"? Each person should define the term individually.

DEFINING EXCELLENCE

Take a minute to consider what "excellence" means *just for you.* There is no right or wrong definition—whatever you decide is correct for you, for your job, now.

In determining your definition of "excellence," remember that the way you personally view excellence affects three things:

- **The outcome of your work**
- **The way you approach problems**
- **The feedback you get from your internal and external customers**

My Definition of Excellence:

____

____

____

____

____

Setting Excellence Goals

Now that you have defined excellence for yourself, put it into action. Think of three goals for achieving excellence in your job.

Keep the following in mind:

- Will you need help or other resources to meet your excellence goals?
- When do you want to meet the goals?
- How will you know when you have met your goals? (That is, what will you use to measure your achievement?)

My Personal Excellence Goals:

1. ______________________________

2. ______________________________

3. ______________________________

Now that you have some personal definitions and goals for excellence, it is time to share these with your team.

Team Definition of ''Excellence''

Discuss your personal definition of excellence with your team. Remember this is only a chance to share information and insight—there are no "better" or "worse" definitions. Can your team achieve consensus on a definition of "excellence"? This team definition may be very different from your personal one, but as an individual you are very different from your team, aren't you?

Team Definition of Excellence:

____

____

____

____

OUR TEAM'S EXCELLENCE GOALS

As before, goals are the next step. Come up with at least three team excellence goals that everyone agrees with. These goals will be the first step in creating a team mission statement.

Team Excellence Goals:

1. ____
2. ____
3. ____
4. ____
5. ____

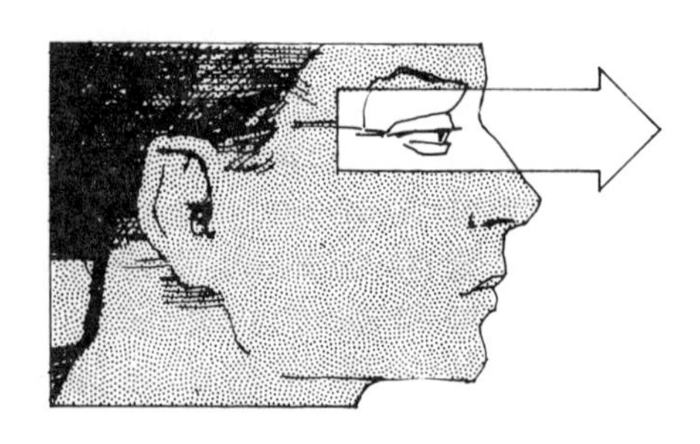

TIP 7

Be Part of the Solution

Remember the saying "If you're not part of the solution, you're part of the problem." Well, this idea applies to teamwork as well as to a number of other solutions in life. The team relies on the input and effort of *all* members. Being "part of the solution" means that you arrive on time, ready and willing to work, to listen to others' ideas, to share your own ideas and to be focused on the work of the team.

The meeting might come at an inconvenient time for you, or you might be bored or unmotivated by the task at hand. At these times your *attitude* really affects your effectiveness. Regardless of the circumstances, only *you* can control your attitude. You have a choice. Make it a goal to let go of whatever is bothering you when you attend team meetings. For that period, willingly contribute to the work of the group.

ARE YOU PART OF THE SOLUTION?

How, specifically, can you use your team meeting time to be sure that you are "part of the solution"?

____

____

____

____

What does being "part of the solution" mean for your team, your department and your organization?

____

____

____

____

Admit Your Mistakes

All people make mistakes. Many people, however, are fearful of admitting they made a mistake because they think they will be punished for it. Total Quality Management allows you to acknowledge your mistakes and learn from them.

> One of Dr. Deming's 14 Points:
>
> **Drive out fear.** Many employees are afraid to ask questions or to take a position, even when they do not understand what their job is or what is right or wrong. They will continue to do things the wrong way, or not do them at all. The economic losses from fear are appalling. To ensure better quality and productivity, people must feel secure.

Remember, once you take the responsibility for an error, you have taken the first step toward correcting it.

ERROR ADMISSION CHECK-UP

Have you ever felt the need to "cover up" a mistake at work because you were afraid of the consequence? ____________________

____

____

____

How did it turn out? ____________________

____

What are some of the benefits of being able to admit mistakes rather than cover them up? ____________________

____

____

____

TIP 9

Do Your Part in the Group Effort

Nothing energizes a team more than feeling that *everyone* is involved and working on the desired outcome. And nothing can sidetrack a good effort more quickly than the feeling that some of the team members are not contributing their fair share.

In a TQM workplace everyone participates to make things better—products and services improve, teamwork becomes more and more effective, and the entire organization is continually energized by the process.

Remember that your personal effectiveness directly influences your organization's overall ability to fulfill its mission—and, ultimately, the performance in the competitive global market.

CHECK THE TEAM'S INVOLVEMENT

Have you ever been uncomfortable with your level of involvement and contribution to your team? (Did you feel you did too *much* or too *little*?) ______________________________

What can you do to increase your effort? ______________________________

What can you do to encourage others to increase their efforts? ______________________________

TIP 10

Learn to Say "I'm Sorry"

Taking responsibility for your actions is an important cornerstone of quality. By learning to say you have made a mistake and are concerned about its impact on others in your team, you accomplish two things:

First, you acknowledge the error and take responsibility for it. This builds trust and respect.

Second, you allow the team to quickly move past the error and get on with the work at hand. Time is not lost finding fault and placing blame.

Sometimes in the early stages of team building it is difficult to be the person who says, "I'm sorry. I made a mistake." Your team has not yet reached a level of trust and support that makes such an admission comfortable. But by going ahead and taking the reponsibility when it is appropriate, you help build the trust and respect that is necessary for the team to work smoothly.

Consider your apology style:

1. Do you feel comfortable accepting sincere apologies?

   ____

2. How do you accept an apology?

   ____

3. How do you prefer to give an apology, face-to-face or in writing?

   ____

4. Do you prefer to apologize in private or in front of others who know you made the error?

   ____

5. How do you think being able to say "I'm sorry" or "I accept your apology" will make your team more effective?

   ____

TIP 11

Learn Something New Each Day

You may think you know just about everything there is to know about your job or your organization. Each day is pretty much the same as the last. You have a routine that you follow, and things happen in a predictable way.

When asked to "learn something new each *day*," you may smile and think, "I'd be lucky to learn something new each *month*!" The fact is that you probably *do* learn something new about your job or your organization every day—you are just unaware of it.

Think About Yesterday:

- How did the day go?

  ____

  ____

- Did you have new problems to solve, customers to serve or memos from your organization to read?

  ____

  ____

- How about your mail or voice mail—did anything new come across your desk?

  ____

  ____

- If you work in manufacturing, how about new people on the job, a new system or method, or new safety rules?

  ____

  ____

Every day you are bombarded with *hundreds* of new thoughts, ideas, rules, products, people and tools.

The trick to making the most of this "informal training" is to be *aware* of it. Make it a point at the beginning of each workday to look for at least one new thing about your job or organization. At the end of the day, review the many transactions and motions of the day and select one of the things that you learned. On some days you may really have to stretch your thinking to find something; on other days it will be hard to narrow it down to just one thing.

Try it out! For the next two work weeks write down something you learned each day. You may want to make this a team project and share your list with the others on your team.

LEARN SOMETHING NEW EACH DAY

Date: Today I Learned . . .

Monday: ____________________

Tuesday: ____________________

Wednesday: ____________________

Thursday: ____________________

Friday: ____________________

Monday: ____________________

Tuesday: ____________________

Wednesday: ____________________

Thursday: ____________________

Friday: ____________________

Notice your growth. Look for opportunities for education and training in your everyday life as well as in formal "lifelong learning" through community colleges, seminars and workshops.

TIP 12

Strive for Zero Defects

Is it reasonable to expect a standard of *zero defects*? Isn't that *impossible*? No. It is very possible. While it may require superior attention to every aspect of your job, it makes sense.

In a Dear Abby syndicated newspaper column, the U.S. Postal Service claimed that its acceptable error rate was about 2%. On the surface that seems to be an excellent goal—98% correct, only 2% missed.

But Dear Abby took the Postal Service to task in a subsequent column, noting the implications of a 2% margin of error.

- 30,000 newborns would be accidentally dropped each year in hospitals.
- 200,000 drug prescriptions would be made up wrong.
- Four days out of each year you would have unsafe drinking water flowing in your pipes.

The fact is that we *expect* a zero defect rate in many occupations. Consider what a higher defect rate would mean to a pilot, a surgeon or a nuclear power plant operator. A zero defect rate is a standard that is attainable for any job—the person behind the job must just care enough to do it right.

OUR ZERO DEFECTS GOALS

What are the implications of your organization's current rate of errors? To answer that question, consider these factors:

- How much does it cost?

____

____

- How many people are inconvenienced or hurt regularly?

____

____

- How much time or material is wasted in a specific period?

____

____

- What, if any, impact is there on the environment or on society?

____

____

- What would a zero defect rate mean in your job?

____

____

____

- Do you feel it is attainable? If you are not sure, what would have to change to make it possible?

____

____

____

TIP 13

Take Charge of Morale

Most people have worked in a situation where the attitude of the workers was described as "low morale" or "morale problems." If you have worked in a failing business, or a company going through a reorganization that required layoffs, or an agency that has had its budget slashed, you know what "low morale" is. Even if you haven't personally experienced it, just watching the evening news about economic downturns and the rising jobless rate shows you what "morale problems" are.

But morale is simply an attitude. Attitudes begin with individuals, and when many individuals share the same attitude, it becomes institutionalized. It takes on "a life of its own" as it is discussed again and again.

People striving to meet a quality standard of continuous improvement define their own morale through the continuing challenge of doing their best.* Morale is high in empowered individuals and teams because *they decide it is*. If morale becomes low or distorted, the team tackles it as a problem to be solved, not a thing to fear.

* For an excellent book on how to get more from your job, use the information in the back of this book to order *Achieving Job Satisfaction*, from the editors of Crisp Publications, Menlo Park, CA. Copyright 1994.

MORALE CHECK

How would you describe the morale of your team right now?

____

____

____

How would you describe your *personal* morale?

____

____

____

What has made it what it is?

____

____

____

Does it need some work?

____

____

____

How could you take full responsibility for raising morale to its highest possible level?

____

____

____

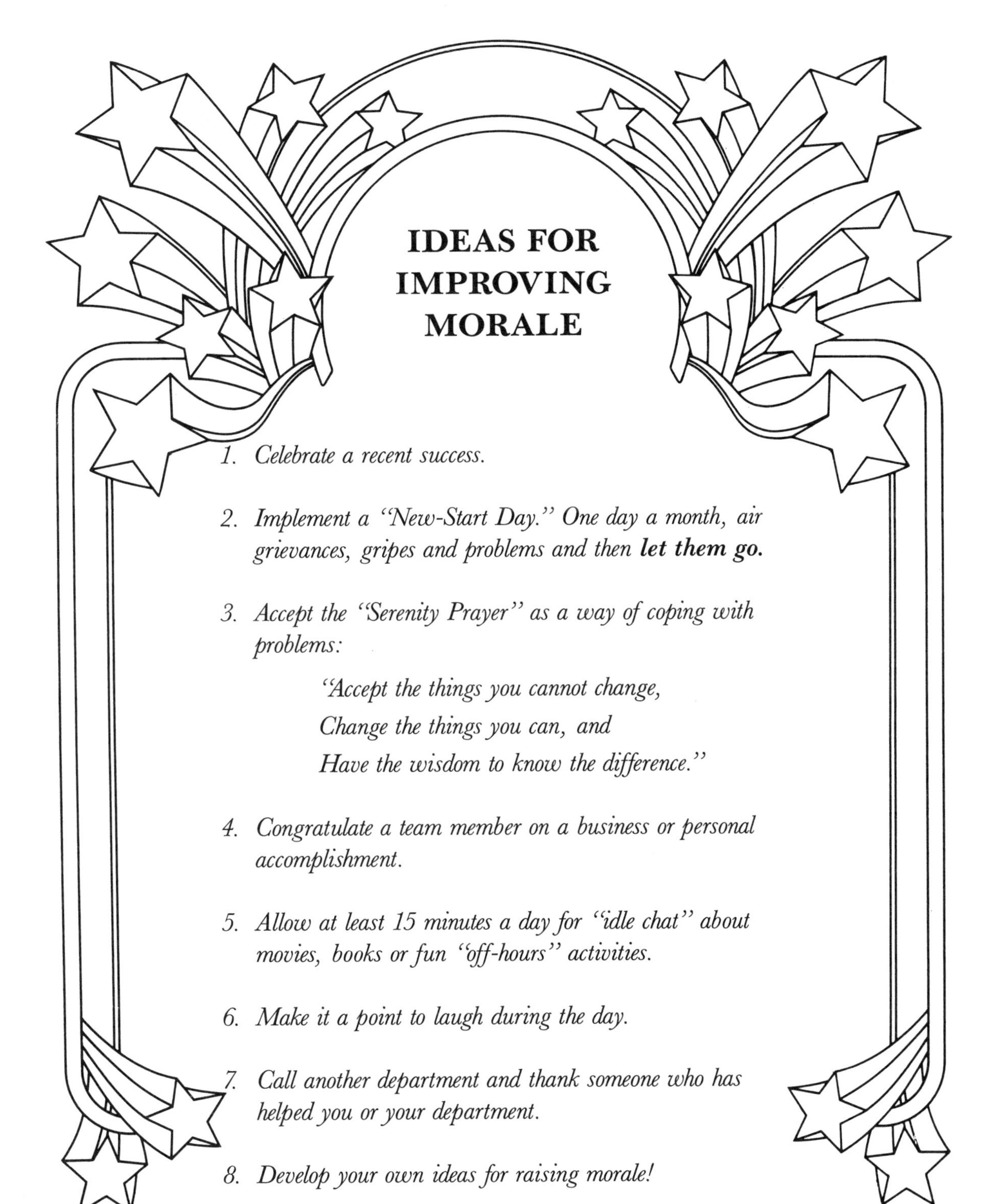

IDEAS FOR IMPROVING MORALE

1. *Celebrate a recent success.*

2. *Implement a "New-Start Day." One day a month, air grievances, gripes and problems and then* **let them go.**

3. *Accept the "Serenity Prayer" as a way of coping with problems:*

   "Accept the things you cannot change,
   Change the things you can, and
   Have the wisdom to know the difference."

4. *Congratulate a team member on a business or personal accomplishment.*

5. *Allow at least 15 minutes a day for "idle chat" about movies, books or fun "off-hours" activities.*

6. *Make it a point to laugh during the day.*

7. *Call another department and thank someone who has helped you or your department.*

8. *Develop your own ideas for raising morale!*

TIP 14

Inspire Trust

What does it take to inspire trust? Trust is built or broken down with every interaction you have with others.

> *To inspire trust:*
>
> ***Keep your commitments***
> ***Tell the truth***
> ***Admit your mistakes***

These seem so simple. Yet many people do *not* inspire trust in others. Why is that?

Everyone has his or her own motivations for not keeping commitments, for lying, or for placing blame on others. But whatever the motivation, this robs people of a valuable asset—the trust of others.

Trust is the cornerstone of teamwork. When everyone on the team knows that the other members can be counted on to put forth their best effort—on time and with care—the level of output from the team is dramatically increased.

TRUST CHECK

How much do you trust the other members of your team or your organization? ______________________

How well are you trusted? ______________________

If you have trust issues with others (or they with you), what will it take to rebuild trust? ______________________

What recommendations do you have for building and inspiring trust in others? ______________________

Offer Suggestions

Have you ever been in a new group or committee where you are asked to brainstorm about a problem and everyone just sits there waiting for someone else to be the first to speak? It's uncomfortable, but not quite as uncomfortable as taking the risk of being the first one to offer an idea.

The fact is that it takes courage to be put in a position of scrutiny—to be the one whom everyone looks at and evaluates. But the rules of brainstorming *do not allow* evaluation during the initial "idea gathering" phase. To get some ideas out on the table for people to consider and build on, someone has to have the courage to speak up.

Do you have an idea or suggestion that you have not offered for fear of rejection? One way to make that first step is to ask someone you trust in the group to provide you with an introduction. For example, ask Mary if she would mention that you have an idea that you would like to share. At the next meeting Mary says, "Linda has a good idea about how we might approach that. Linda, why don't you tell everyone your plan for cutting mail costs?"

Try it the next time you have a chance. As your team works together and you increase your trust and support within the group, it will become easier and easier to risk the possible rejection of your suggestions. You will become more comfortable with letting your idea become a springboard for the final decision that, through consensus, offers the best solution to the problem.

IDEA-OFFERING CHECK-UP

The following is an idea I have wanted to share with my team: ________________________________

____

____

____

I will ask ____________________ to provide an introduction for me at our next meeting.

TIP 16

Look for Opportunities in Losses or Mistakes

A proverb says, "When a door is closed, a window opens." But sometimes it is hard to accept a loss or to admit a mistake. We wish that it had never happened; in some cases we sink into depression or denial to avoid accepting the loss or guilt.

But as the proverb asserts, there is always something positive that results from a loss or mistake. As you know, many profound discoveries in medicine and science were the result of a mistake or wrong conclusion. In our personal lives we meet and are influenced by people we encounter in unhappy circumstances. And we can learn to accept things we never thought we could.

In your work there will be times when you feel very wronged. You will be angry that your team members will not go along with an idea or a process that you offer. You may have to support something that you don't completely agree with. And you may have to help "pick up the pieces" when someone makes a mistake that you saw coming.

In every problem there is an opportunity. The trick is to believe it first, and then to look for the opportunity.

OPPORTUNITY CHECK

Think of a significant loss or mistake that you have had to endure.

Name at least three opportunities or good things that have come to you as a result of the loss.

____
____
____
____
____
____

Describe people that you met, support that you received, or a chance to make changes that would not have happened if the loss or mistake hadn't occurred.

____
____
____
____
____
____

In your team take the time and effort to identify the opportunities in losses or mistakes that happen. *These opportunities are the gateways to continuous improvement.*

____
____
____
____
____
____

TIP 17

Accept Revision As Proof That Someone Cares

Most people do not welcome change. Change is scary. It involves all sorts of unknowns and new problems that will require attention. Even in really bad situations, people will often stick with the known rather than the unknown, which may be even more horrible.

Revision appears to imply a mistake. "If this was so wonderful, how come they are revising it?" The revision process is open to scrutiny and nit-picking because the original is now viewed with skepticism.

Both change and revision, however, are welcome in the TQM organization. Just as we must view problems as desirable and helpful in continuous improvement, we need to view change as a reminder that someone cares enough to make an effort to improve.

ACCEPTANCE OF CHANGE CHECK-UP

When have you had to accept change or revision in your job?

____

____

____

How did you feel about it?

____

____

Did you wish you could keep doing things "the old way," or were you glad that the change was coming?

____

____

____

Do others around you welcome change or resent the additional training and effort it requires?

____

____

____

How would you explain the concept of change as "proof that someone cares" to another person?

____

____

____

TIP 18

Don't Gossip or Spread Rumors

One of the most powerful systems in any organization is the "grapevine." Through gossip and secondhand information you hear who's going to be hired or fired, what the new product will be, or what sweeping policy changes are being discussed at the senior management level.

The only problem with this powerful system is that it is not very accurate. Although there is usually *some truth* to grapevine rumors—maybe personnel changes *are* being considered—the rumors are seldom wholly accurate. The incorrect and misleading parts of the story often alarm and confuse people unnecessarily.

Gossip needs to be curtailed to improve the quality of both your workplace and your product. Effective teams are built on trust and respect. It is damaging to the team as well as the individual when gossip and innuendos are allowed to circulate without anyone checking the facts.

What would you do, though, when you *do* check the facts, and the facts substantiate the gossip? Well, that's a personal decision, but a good rule of thumb is to determine whether the situation is relevant to the workplace or is a purely personal matter. In situations where your workplace may be affected (such as a team member's substance abuse on the job), your best recourse is to either talk directly with the team member in question or bring the *facts as you know them* to the attention of your supervisor.

CHECKING OUT THE GOSSIP MILL

What kinds of gossip or rumors are common in your workplace?

____

____

____

What do you usually do to get the facts?

____

____

____

How do you think gossip or rumor has affected your workplace? Can you think of specific examples?

____

____

____

How would you handle a situation where you knew about a co-worker's theft or substance abuse on the job?

____

____

____

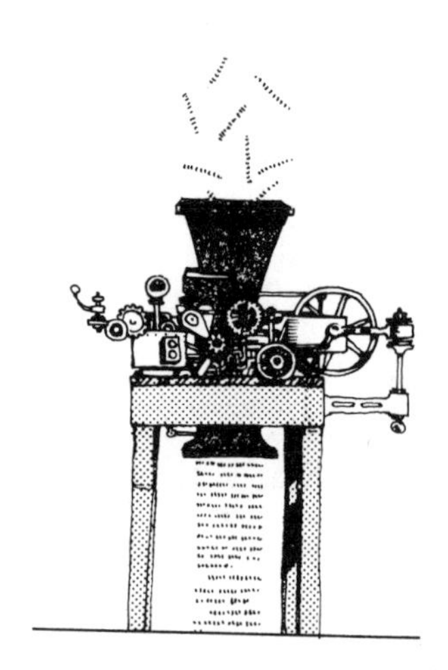

SECTION 2

Improve Teamwork and Commitment

TIP 19

Know Your Organization's Mission

Total Quality Management organizations are driven by the concept "constancy of purpose." Constancy of purpose means that everyone knows where the organization is headed and what its overall goals and objectives are.

One method that organizations use to describe their purpose is the "mission statement." The mission statement provides you with a map of the territory; reading it can help you understand the direction and priorities of your organization.*

A clear, understandable mission gives you the framework for your team's goals. Does your organization include "innovation" in its mission? Well, then research and development of new products and services are probably priorities. Is "increasing our market presence" a part of the mission? That would signal marketing and customer service as important factors.

Some mission statements are not as clearly defined as others. Ask for clarification. "Constancy of purpose" requires that the decisions and actions of the *entire organization* (not just management) be in line with the organization's mission. If you cannot understand the mission, it's pretty difficult to live it.

Your organization's mission enables you to base your decisions and actions on a reliable "road map" of goals and expectations.

* If your team needs help clarifying its mission, order *Organizational Vision, Values and Mission,* by Cynthia Scott, Dennis Jaffe and Glenn Tobe. Crisp Publications, Menlo Park, CA. Copyright 1994.

CLARIFY YOUR TEAM'S MISSION

What is your organization's mission statement? ______________________________

What does it mean to *your* job? ______________________________

What are the priorities of the organization? ______________________________

How does your job rank in relation to the organizational priorities? ______________________________

TIP 20

Know Your Team's Goals

Your team's goals are the measure by which you judge your team's success. Your goals should include both general and specific objectives that spell out the *what, why, how, when* and *who* of your team's projects.

A *general* goal is an overall statement of what you hope to accomplish as a team.

A general team goal:

"We will provide ideas and direction for making the product introduction of the XV-5000 the most successful in our company's history."

A *specific* goal provides a *method* of working that meets the needs of your team.

A specific team goal:

"Each time a team decision is required, we will hear the opinion of each team member before we make a choice."

IDENTIFY YOUR TEAM GOALS

What are your team's goals, both general and specific? ______________________________

How many goals do you need? ______________________________

How do your goals correspond to your organization's mission statement? ______________________________

Have you changed and adapted your goals as situations have changed? ______________________________

What *unspoken* goals are you operating with at this time? ______________________________

TIP 21

Start and End Team Meetings on Time

Most people resent attending meetings that start late and then seem to go on forever. The value of the meeting is lost when team members are checking their watches and thinking about what they should be doing back at their work stations.

Make it a point to start all meetings on time. Regardless of who is present and who isn't, begin. People who come in late will have to take the responsibility for finding out what happened *at a later time*. Do not stop the meeting to repeat for latecomers.

Make an agenda and *stick to it*. If you do not get through the entire agenda, schedule another meeting or assign the items to team members who will work on them and report back at the next meeting.

End the meeting *right on time*. Avoid long reviews and conclusions, but do take time to create Action Plans and make sure that everyone knows what is expected of them. Schedule the next meeting and ask for agenda items.

TEAM MEETING TIME CHECK-UP

How is your team doing in starting and stopping meetings on time? ______________________

Do you generally follow the agreed-upon time frame? ______________________

Do you usually make and stick with an agenda? ______________________

How could you make your team meetings more effective and efficient? ______________________

TIP 22

Be Tough on Problems—Soft on People

Problems are important. They point out where improvement is needed. All teams must learn to avoid blaming others or personalizing a problem when it is brought to light. The energy of your team is better spent *solving* the problem and seeking improvement.

> ***Deming's 85-15 Rule***
>
> *Most people work in a system over which they have little control. It is up to management to improve the system rather than point fingers at people when problems occur. Dr. Deming maintains that systems are responsible for 85% of the problems in organizations—people for only 15%. The burden of improvement is on the management of the organization to create a system that serves the people who work within it.*

Thus, by being tough on problems and soft on its people, an organization maintains its greatest resource for dealing with whatever obstacles and dilemmas it may encounter.

CHECKING OUT THE 85-15 RULE

What does it mean to be "tough on problems, soft on people"? ____________________

Does an example come to mind? ____________________

Do you agree with Deming that 85% of problems are a result of "the system"? ____________________

Can you think of an example from your own experience? ____________________

Prepare for "Storming" Times

In 1955 Bruce Tuckman defined the Four Stages of Group Development as:

FORMING ➡ STORMING ➡ NORMING ➡ PERFORMING

In the early stage (forming) everyone is generally polite and conflict is mostly avoided.

The second stage, "storming," is one of the most difficult periods in the life of a team. After the excitement and pride of forming the group, the realization of what the task is and how difficult it may be overwhelms many team members. In the "storming" stage you may feel that the general mood of the team is testy, blameful or overzealous. In this stage the team may exhibit the following:

- Resistance to quality improvement; a yearning to go back to the "old way"
- Concern about the project's chance for success
- Dissention and argument over trivial matters
- Defensiveness and competition among members
- Establishing unrealistic goals or complaining about excessive work and responsibility

While this stage feels unproductive and at times you may wonder if any of your team goals will be met, remember that this is a *normal process*. Teams who weather this period move into the "norming" phase where team guidelines and ground rules form the basis for attention to task. The final phase, "performing," is the reward for your patience. In this period your team will be capable of making up for much of the time that was "lost" getting the team to work together.

IDENTIFY THE STAGE YOUR GROUP IS IN

Where would you put your team in Tuckman's Four Stages of Group Development?

____

____

____

____

Have you experienced the "storming" stage?

____

____

____

____

What ideas for weathering this stage can you share with your team?

____

____

____

____

TIP 24

Help Your Group Reach Consensus

What does it take to "reach consensus?" Does everyone have to heartily endorse the idea, or is it still consensus if some people just "give in" to end a long, boring standoff? Well, hopefully your team will learn to achieve consensus without having to demand absolute endorsement or to settle for "majority rule." If even a slim margin wins, all must go along with the choice. But in your team setting, you can achieve a higher level of group decision making through **consensus**.

Consensus simply means that all voices have been heard, all opinions are out in the open, and the individuals of the team have come to a group decision. This means that not every decision will go exactly as everyone wants. Sometimes compromises will help, sometimes the group needs more information, and sometimes the decision must be tabled while members think it over or consult other sources.

Five Ways to Reach Group Consensus

1. Take time to hear from every member.
2. Write down the options so everyone can remember what has been suggested.
3. Remind the group that simple "majority rule" is not an option.
4. Point out possible compromises or other ideas.
5. Offer to help with "trial runs" or "models" of different ideas if more information is needed.

If *everyone* on the team takes responsibility for reaching consensus, the spirit of solving the problem or completing the task will have a much better chance of overcoming each individual's need to "be right."

CONSENSUS CHECK-UP

How easily does your team reach consensus? ______________________

What can you do to make each member an integral part of the decision-making process? ______________________

If the members of your team do not willingly compromise, what adjustments can you make in the process to make compromise easier? ______________________

TIP 25 Appreciate Your Team's Diversity

With the advent of fast, relatively inexpensive international travel, people are immigrating to other countries in ever-increasing numbers. Companies (and countries) now have the challenge to create "unity of purpose" from a culturally diverse group of people.

The greatest effects of diversity are often on communication. We know that men and women have different communication patterns. Ethnic, religious, and regional cultures also have different ways of communicating. When a person makes an important point, for instance, one culture may dictate that the person speak up in a loud and commanding voice, while another culture may value the person who speaks slowly in a soft voice.

Consider a few of the differences your team must accept, build upon and help others to accept if it is to achieve its full potential:

- Country of origin
- Native language
- Gender
- Race
- Religion
- Education and literacy
- Sociocultural background
- Math skills
- Work experience
- Age

DIVERSITY BENEFITS QUICK-CHECK

In what ways is the diversity of your team members a *positive force* for your team? Brainstorm some ideas.

____

____

____

____

____

TIP 26

Develop an Effective Problem-Solving Process

There are many problem-solving processes that generate ideas and solutions. One simple and effective problem-solving model is the Six-Step Method:

SIX-STEP PROBLEM-SOLVING METHOD

1. **Define the Problem.** Be as specific as possible in defining all aspects of the problem.

2. **Brainstorm Possible Causes.** As a group, come up with as many possible causes as you can. Avoid fault finding; focus on objective reasons why the problem has occurred.

3. **Analyze the Data.** Gather as much data as you can about the existing condition. Carefully review the data and look for trends, patterns and cause-and-effect situations.

4. **Brainstorm Possible Solutions.** Generate as many alternative solutions as possible. Avoid passing judgment about which solutions will or will not work.

5. **Reach Consensus on Solutions.** Review each of the possible solutions and list the benefits and costs of each one. Select the best (and next best) solution through consensus. Remember that action can follow more smoothly once consensus is reached.

6. **Develop an Action Plan.** Clearly define your Action Plan through each step. The Action Plan should include *what* will be done, *who* will do it and *when* it will be completed.

PROBLEM-SOLVING CHECK-UP

Practice this problem-solving method using a real (or hypothetical) problem facing your team right now:

What is the problem you need to solve?

____

____

____

Apply the six steps to the problem (this may take a few meetings to accomplish).

____

____

____

Critique your team's use of the model. What steps were most helpful?

____

____

____

Modify the process to meet the needs of your team more realistically.

____

____

____

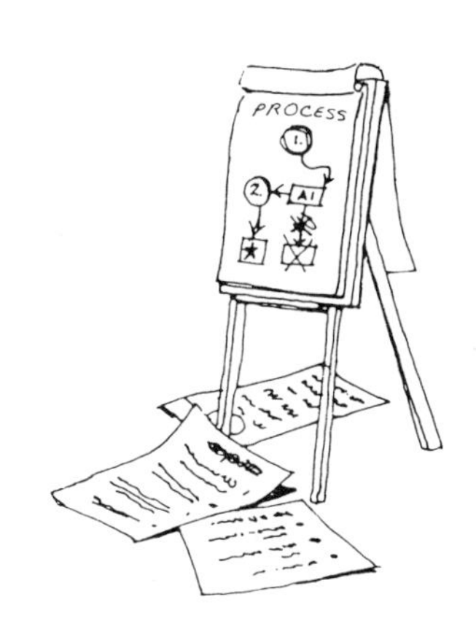

TIP 27

Celebrate Your Success

Take the time and effort to celebrate the successes of your team. Each member should be kept up to date when performance goals are met and should share in the acknowledgment and satisfaction of a job well done.

Over the past 50 years behavioral scientists have studied what motivates people—what causes an increase or decrease in performance. The studies clearly show that when people are acknowledged and rewarded for something they have done, they will want to do it again. When they are ignored or punished, they avoid that behavior.

When your team does something great, meets a tough deadline or solves a sticky problem in an especially ingenious way, celebrate! Acknowledge and reward yourselves. You will find that you are much more eager to tackle the next "impossible task" when you have taken time to celebrate the success of the moment.

PLAN A CELEBRATION

What particularly difficult task is your team working on right now?

____

____

____

____

What would be an appropriate and satisfying celebration when you complete that task successfully?

____

____

____

____

CELEBRATE SUCCESS

- *Create a bulletin board in the coffee room or entry lobby to display photos or mementos of successful teams and their accomplishments.*
- *Have a little party or potluck lunch.*
- *Write an article for a newsletter, magazine or the local paper.*
- *Decorate your offices or work area for a day.*
- *Everyone chip in and buy your team a plaque or plant.*
- *Bring in spouses, children, and friends for a demonstration or a reception.*
- *Take some well-earned time off after an especially difficult task is successfully completed.*
- *Come up with a celebration idea that you and your team would enjoy, and then* ***do it!***

TIP 28

Use Open-Ended Questions

The best conversationalists are those who ask open-ended questions that give the other person a chance to fully explore and explain his or her point of view. Open-ended questions elicit participation.

In teams that have a high participation level, you will notice that the members are skilled in asking open-ended questions.

HOW TO RECOGNIZE AN OPEN-ENDED QUESTION

Open-Ended Questions Begin With:

What . . . ? *Why . . . ?*

Where . . . ? *How . . . ?*

Open-ended questions require an answer beyond a simple "yes" or "no."

Asking open-ended questions is a *skill* that requires practice, but it will soon become a *habit* that will benefit you as an individual and as a member of your team.

OPEN-ENDED QUESTION QUICK-CHECK

Think of possible open-ended questions that *you* might use to:

- Start a discussion ____________________
  ____
- Ask a team member for his or her opinion ____________________
  ____
- Bring the conversation back on track ____________________
  ____

Test your questions by checking if any could be answered with a simple "yes" or "no."

TIP 29

Help with Your Team's "Chores"

Teams that work *well* are those that work *together.* There are always tasks that most people do not enjoy doing, but they must be done. In TQM organizations these tasks are shared equally among the members of the team. Teams avoid assigning tasks; they ask for volunteers instead. In on-going assignments, such as note taking, it is good to design a rotation system so that everyone shares the chores equally.

In non-TQM organizations the unpleasant tasks were often delegated to those with "lesser status." You knew hierarchy and power structure by who was expected to make the coffee and who was responsible for taking notes. Sex discrimination was often apparent. Women were expected to assume tasks (such as typing up the notes) because they were women; men were expected to do other tasks (such as moving furniture) because they were men.

In your group, offer to do your share of all of the necessary tasks. You need not *always* offer, but be willing to assume responsibility whenever you can. And keep in mind that we perpetuate the stereotypes that others hold of us when we consistently choose tasks that are "conventional" for our gender, age, position or experience.

HOW DOES YOUR TEAM DIVIDE CHORES?

How are the "chores" usually handled in your team? ______________________________

____

Do the same people volunteer again and again while some members *never* seem to help out? ______________________________

____

____

Do you fall into conventional stereotypes of "women's work" vs. "men's work" in chore assignments? ______________________________

____

____

What can you do as an individual and as a team to handle the chores more equitably? ______________________________

____

____

TIP 30

Share Ideas as Well as Problems

In TQM organizations problems are sought out; they are highly regarded as opportunities for continuous improvement. However, problems alone will not create improvement. You need *ideas* to solve problems. Your team needs *everyone's* ideas to do the best possible job.

Some team members see their job as "problem spotters." They bring only problems to the group, expecting others to solve them. Other people show up only to attack the problems that others have brought. They have a "blue sky" approach that tries to avoid problems by not admitting that any exist.

The team needs everyone to bring *both* problems and ideas to the table. Brainstorming works best when everyone shares the responsibility for generating ideas and solving the problems.

IDEAS AND PROBLEMS CHECK-UP

Consider your team:

Do you have "problem spotters" and "blue sky" people? ______________________________

What can you do as a team to give everyone the chance to bring *both* problems and ideas to the group? ______________________________

Are you following brainstorming guidelines when attacking a problem—that is, generating as many ideas as possible before selecting a possible solution? ______________________________

How does your team make sure that everyone's ideas are heard? ______________________________

TIP 31

Use "Creative Dissatisfaction" as an Incentive

Problems are the lifeblood of quality improvement. If everything were perfect, we would have no incentive to improve. But many people are uncomfortable with problems; they want them to "go away." In TQM organizations, problems are sought after. They are highly prized because they provide the riddle to solve, the means to a better end.

Your team will be dealing with the philosophy of "continuous improvement," which is based on the concept of "creative dissatisfaction."

In other words, even when things are OK, there is always room for improvement. Even before a customer complains or a system breaks down, you can use creative dissatisfaction to see that things could be better. When you find something that could be improved, you have *created a problem*. Although this seems crazy to those who have avoided "making waves" or being labeled as "troublemakers," this is the way that continuous improvement happens. Problems become as important as solutions.

In your TQM team, instead of dodging problems, you will view them as:

1. Improvement and learning opportunities
2. Continuous improvement potential
3. A natural part of the improvement process
4. Easily solved without blame
5. Best solved in groups
6. Best solved *as soon as possible*

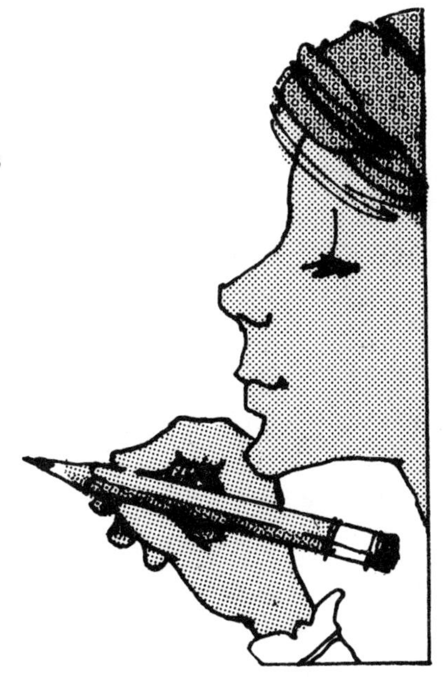

DO YOU USE CREATIVE DISSATISFACTION?

What problems can you uncover through "creative dissatisfaction" with the way things are in your team or work area?

____

____

____

____

____

What opportunities for improvement can you see in these problems?

____

____

____

____

____

TIP 32

Ignore Complaining

Some people see team meetings as "group therapy," their opportunity to complain about everything from the parking situation to the world situation. Often other team members feel that they must address these complaints and remarks because not to do so would be to ignore the complainer.

Your team meetings, however, are for problem solving in a commitment to continuous improvement. They are not personal gripe sessions for members.

The best way to avoid getting bogged down in chronic complaining and blaming is to agree not to focus on those issues. If a team member has a complaint that can be appropriately addressed by the team, it should be placed on the agenda. If the complaint is inappropriate to the work of the team (a personal problem, a global problem over which you have no control, etc.), it should be identified as such and ignored.

Do not allow your team meetings to become sessions where members simply "vent their feelings." Although anger will surface during the work of the team, the agenda needs to focus on generating ideas and solving problems to make team meetings productive for all the members.

CHECK YOUR TIME WASTERS

How does your team control complaining, inappropriate remarks and other time wasters? ______________________________

Do you feel that the work of your team takes priority over complaints? ______________________________

How do you handle complaints that are beyond the control of your team? ______________________________

Listen Respectfully to Each Team Member

American workers are not used to being formally rated by their peers. The only people who "matter" when it comes to granting raises and promotions are those at the next level—the supervisors and managers who watch and rank the performance of their employees.

But in a self-managed team setting, this will change. You need to learn to listen to each other with the same intensity and concern that you would give your "boss." These team members *are* your bosses—or will be someday. You will, in turn, be their boss as well. You will be listened to and given the same consideration by your team members as by the person who oversees the work of your group for senior management.

What a responsibility! Before, you had to concern yourself with the wishes and dictates of just *one* boss. Now you have an entire team of people listening to you, watching you, evaluating your performance. Don't worry, though; the only people who will find this attention uncomfortable are those who have something to hide. *You* will be energized by getting your good ideas implemented, by having your problems and concerns given the attention they deserve, and by helping the team and each of its members reach goals that may have seemed extraordinary just a few years ago.

TEAM MEMBER PERFORMANCE CHECK-UP

How do you think your team members would rate your performance if they were considering you for a promotion?

____

____

____

____

What areas do you need to improve in?

____

____

What are your strong areas?

____

____

How do you feel about rating your team members' performance?

____

____

Empathize with Other Team Members' Feelings

An old saying goes, "Don't pass judgment until you have walked a mile in another person's shoes."

Expressing empathy lets the other person know that you are aware of his or her feelings and that you respect those feelings. Examples of empathetic expressions are "Let me see if I understand what you mean . . ." or "I can see that this is not what you had in mind; what do you think should be done?" In short, let the other team member know that *you* know their concern. Don't just ignore the feelings or tell the person to feel or act differently.

A caring, empathetic atmosphere makes it easier for honesty and frankness to be the norm in your team meetings.

Addressing others' feelings and concerns with empathy:

- **Helps reduce strong emotions.** It's hard to hang on to strong emotions that have been expressed.
- **Encourages other people to listen to you.** You can expect a similar level of empathy in return.
- **Relieves anxiety in the team.** Once feelings are out in the open, people can deal with them and the tension is relieved.

SHOWING EMPATHY QUICK-CHECK

How would you deal empathetically with a team member who announced that she felt that everyone else on the team was "ganging up" on her and that her ideas were not given the consideration they deserved? (Remember, it doesn't matter whether her ideas are usually off-base or on-target—your response to her feelings of exclusion would be the same.)

____

____

____

____

TIP 35

Put into Practice "Actions Speak Louder than Words"

The real value of the work of your team lies in its actions, not its words. Although we use words to communicate action, don't make the mistake of *substituting* words for action.

Your Action Plans can be compared to the paycheck that you receive for your work. If it is just a piece of paper without any value behind it, it is worthless. Just as you expect your employer to put money in the bank to cover your paycheck, your Action Plans should have concrete action behind them to get the job done. Coming up with great ideas is only the *beginning*. The real work is in trying out your ideas and solving the problem or improving the system.

Develop clearly stated Action Plans so that every team member leaves the meeting knowing:

1. **What action steps have been agreed on.** What needs to be done?
2. **Who will do each step.** Who is responsible for what?
3. **When each step must be completed.** What are the deadlines?

ARE YOU USING AN ACTION PLAN?

Does your team have a problem or project that could benefit from developing an Action Plan to put words into action?

____
____
____
____

Check the section on Action Plans at the front of this book for more ideas on making and using Action Plans.

____
____
____
____

Find at Least One More Solution to Every Problem

Roger von Oech's wonderful books on creativity, *A Whack on the Side of the Head* and *A Kick in the Seat of the Pants,* are excellent sources of ideas for how to spark creative problem solving in your team.

One of Mr. von Oech's suggestions is to look for the "second right answer." This means that you do not stop when you have found a possible solution. You search for another, just as valid *second* solution. Consider the wisdom of this: Your team is excited about a solution that you have come up with on paper, something that has never been tried. But the first time you try it out—dismal failure. If you have a *second* solution, you can quickly switch gears and move on. If you do not, you must regroup and start all over again.

Or another scenario: Your team has come up with a great idea, but it must be approved by management. You know budgets are tight, but you are hoping that your proposal will win them over. It doesn't. With your *second* solution (probably a more modest proposal), you are able to provide an alternative that you both can live with. You may not get *everything,* but all of the time and effort you put into your first proposal was not a total waste either.

The final argument for the "second right answer" is that often by stretching your thinking beyond the obvious first answer, you may actually find a *superior* second answer. Sometimes the first thing that comes to mind is only the *easiest,* not the *best*.

FIND A "SECOND RIGHT ANSWER"

Could your team benefit by searching for a "second right answer" to a problem or project that you are working on right now? ______________________

What will you look for in the second answer? ______________________

Can you think of a time when having a second idea would have served your team well? ______________________

SECTION 3

Focus on Customers and Service

TIP 37

Define the Term "Customer"

Many organizations narrowly define their customer as just the person or organization that ultimately pays for and uses their product or service. That's a big mistake.

In a Total Quality system *any user* of your department's product or service is considered a "customer." Even people *within* your own company or agency are your "customers." TQM distinguishes people within your organization as "internal" customers and people outside the organization as "external" customers. Why the distinction? Well, even though *both* are worthy of your service and commitment, you will have different procedures for handling external and internal customer service problems or concerns.

Take a minute to write down three external customers for your organization. This should be easy. Who is the end user or recipient of your products or services?

Now take a few more minutes to write down three internal customers in your company or agency. Is this more difficult? (*Hint:* Think of the people who rely on the work of your department to get their own work done.)

WHO ARE YOUR CUSTOMERS?

Once you have identified your "external" and "internal" customers, you know who will be the target of the first-class service attitude and commitment of your team.

Our external customers:

1. ______________________________
2. ______________________________
3. ______________________________

Our internal customers:

1. ______________________________
2. ______________________________
3. ______________________________

Share Your Expertise

When you work in a team environment, the higher quality of ideas and the increased amount of work output is often attributed to a concept called "synergy." Synergy is "a combined or cooperative action that results in a total effect that is greater than the sum of the parts."

In short, 1 + 1 + 1 + 1 = 6

One of the ways that synergy works is through people sharing their expertise. If you are an expert in some aspect of your team's work, offer to spread that expertise to other members of your team through training. Are you especially versatile in a computer software program, or do you have some creative shortcuts for accomplishing a tedious task? Train other members of your team. This results in two benefits:

1. You are freed from the responsibility of being called on each time something happens or changes that requires this expertise. You have created your own "backup system."

2. Your team as a whole becomes more valuable, more expert, more fun to work with because everyone shares a common knowledge base from which you can brainstorm and be creative.

CAN YOU SHARE YOUR EXPERTISE?

Think of one or two areas of expertise in which you could train other members of your team.

____

____

____

Are there members who have knowledge or skills that *you* would like to know?

____

____

____

TIP 39

Use Your Judgment

Nordstrom is a Seattle-based specialty store known for its excellent customer service. People who shop at Nordstrom expect a superior level of service, and they know that the people in the organization will meet their expectations.

Given this service commitment, it should not be surprising that the Nordstrom Employee Handbook states only one rule:

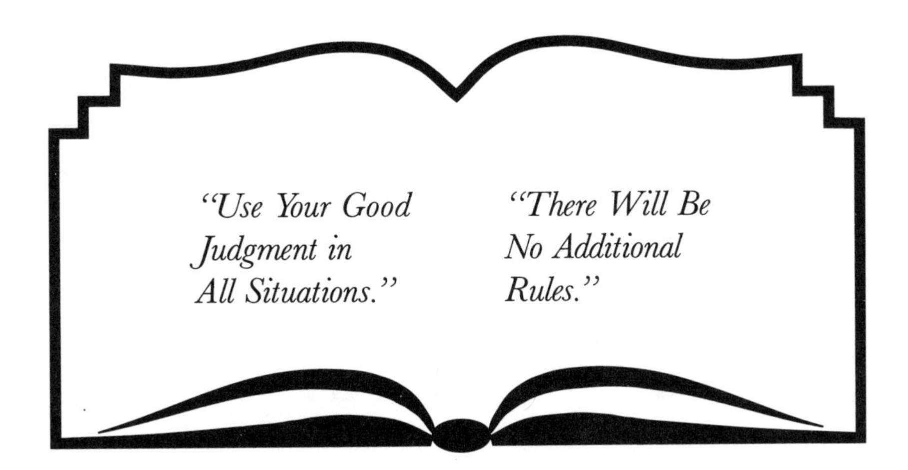

Nordstrom regularly posts the highest sales per square foot of store space in the retail industry. So you see, giving people the responsibility for doing what they think is best is not only the right thing, it is profitable as well.

Being able to do the right thing according to your own best judgment makes your job more interesting and meaningful. It is empowering to tackle and solve a tough problem. It gives you a good feeling when you offer to help out a customer and he or she is satisfied.

CHECK YOUR JUDGMENT

What parts of your job require you to use your judgment to "do the right thing"?

____

____

____

How do you feel about this responsibility?

____

____

____

Are there areas in your job description where you would like to have even *more* responsibility?

____

____

____

Can you think of an example of when you used your best judgment to solve a problem? How did it turn out?

____

____

____

TIP 40

Distinguish Between Your "Job" and Your "Work"

Have you ever considered the difference between your "job" and your "work"? Your "job" can suffer because of your preoccupation with your "work." Suppose you are a sales clerk in a clothing store. For the next 20 minutes your *work* is to straighten up the sweaters on a sale table—but your *job* is to create an environment that will make customers want to buy the sweaters. You can see that it would not be in the best interest of your *job* to push away a customer who is digging through your neatly stacked piles to find the right size. But wait a minute! This customer is ruining all of your hard *work*.

Even employees who don't have direct contact with *external* customers have contact with *internal* customers in their organization. They, too, must consider the possible conflict between their "job" and their "work."

JOB VERSUS WORK CHECK-UP

What is your *job*? (That is, what is the reason that you are employed by this organization?)

____

____

What is your *work*? (That is, what do you do to fill the hours you are at work?)

____

____

Can you think of times when you had *work* that got in the way of your *job*—that is, you had to do something in just one particular way or within a very short time frame, interfering with your *job* of giving good service?

____

____

Brainstorm in your team about "work" policies and practices that might be changed to allow you to do your "job" more effectively.

____

____

TIP 41

Remember, Everyone *Has* and *Is* a Customer

TQM advances the concept that there are both "external" and "internal" customers. Your internal customers are the people who work inside your organization. Regardless of where they are located, the people who depend on you and the work you do to complete their own work are *your customers*.

Quality-conscious organizations are finding that paying attention to internal customers improves their service to the external customers.

At Dun & Bradstreet, a financial company, internal and external customers are identified by asking two questions:

1. Where does my work go?

2. Who is my work important to?

HOW CAN YOU IMPROVE CUSTOMER SERVICE?

Who is my work important to? ______________________________

How could you improve your service to them? (Ask them. Listen to their ideas.) ______________________________

How could you coach the people to whom *you* are a customer to meet your needs better? ______________________________

TIP 42

Develop Friendly Relationships

Everyone must deal with people from other departments or entities. Even if you work in a very small company or agency, you work with particular people on a continuing basis, people in the mail room or the post office, your purchasing department or direct vendors, and, of course, those in payroll.

TQM organizations value the informal relationships between people as well as the formal ones. Developing a friendly relationship, knowing someone by name and acknowledging him or her as a person as well as work contact, establishes a link that will help you do your job. Too many people use only the power of their position to get things done—or problems solved.

Most of us have known people at work who are great contacts. They seem to know everything and everyone in the organization, and they can cut through red tape and bureaucracy and get to the bottom of things. What do these people have? Power. How did they get it? By being friendly, concerned, available and helpful to the people that they now have relationships with. Our work lives are sterile enough without our making them more so.

SIX WAYS TO IMPROVE INTERDEPARTMENTAL COOPERATION

1. Be friendly.
2. Be helpful.
3. Ask names and give your name.
4. Pay compliments when they are due.
5. Remember to thank those who help you out.
6. And, of course, return a favor whenever possible.

INTERDEPARTMENTAL COOPERATION CHECK-UP

Name the people and departments that you deal with on an ongoing basis.

____

____

How do you make yourself more than just a face or voice on the phone to these people?

____

____

What value can you see in expanding your friendly contacts with other departments in your organization?

____

____

What specific ideas can you offer for building friendly relationships with people you work with?

____

____

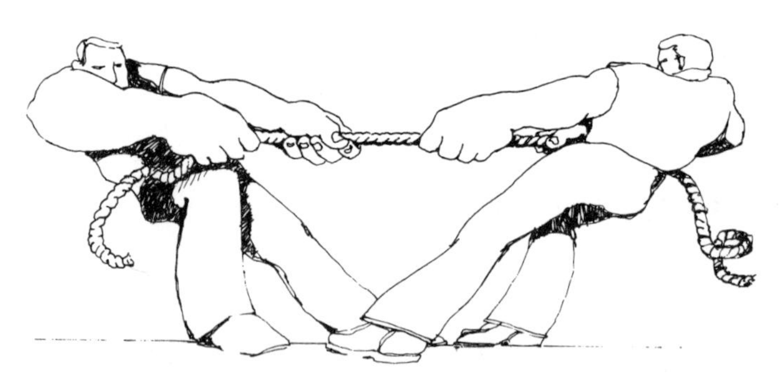

THIS IS NOT GOING TO GET THEM ANYWHERE!

TIP 43

Help When There's a Time Crunch

In our fast-paced work world it seems that there is never enough time. We all appreciate it when someone steps up to help when a time crunch makes finishing a task seem impossible. People who offer help when it is needed are the people who can expect help when the inevitable deadline hits them.

Of course, the best way to deal with looming deadlines is to be organized and prepared in the first place. Are you comfortable with the way you handle the everyday "time bandits" in your job? These "bandits" include reading mail and memos, handling customer problems, and doing necessary paperwork. Do you have some ideas for streamlining these day-in, day-out tasks?

One of the best ways to help alleviate time crunches in your department is to give some thought *beforehand* to improving everyone's efficiency; share your ideas and listen to the ideas of others.

Remember, the "way we've always done it" does *not* necessarily mean "the best way it can be done."

CHECKING OUT YOUR TIME CRUNCHES

How do you know when there's a time crunch for other members of your team?

____

____

What kind of help can you offer?

____

____

How does your team avoid time crunches and bottlenecks in the first place?

____

____

TIP 44

Listen Actively to Your Customers

The first step in meeting—and exceeding—your customers' needs is to *listen* to them.

"Active listening" focuses on:

1. **What we hear**
2. **What we understand**
3. **What we remember**

Most of us *actively* listen to only about 25% of what we hear; the other 75% is lost. To provide excellent service to our customers, we need to know as much as we can about what they want, how they want it, when they want it, what they expect to pay for it, how long they expect to wait, and anything else they expect.

Listening is a skill that improves the more you practice. The listener's advantage is that most people speak about 125 to 150 words per minute, but we can listen to up to 450 words per minute. Use that extra time to identify the speaker's main points and consciously memorize them.

ARE YOU AN ACTIVE LISTENER?

What opportunities do you have for strengthening your active listening skills? ______________________________

How would improving your listening and memory benefit you, your customers and your organization? ______________________________

Make two listening improvement goals that you can actively work on and evaluate in the next few weeks: ______________________________

TIP 45

Use Customers' Names

A person's name is his or her favorite sound. Most people appreciate it when you make the effort to remember and use their name.

Here are a few tips for remembering names:

1. **Actively listen when you are introduced.** Check with the person to be sure you heard his or her name correctly. If it is an unusual name, ask how it is spelled. Use the name in conversation as soon as possible to imprint it in your memory.

2. **Concentrate on the person.** We have all had the unnerving experience of being introduced to someone and two minutes later realizing we did not hear the person's name. Be alert and concentrate on the face and features of the person you are being introduced to.

3. **Use association tricks to recall the name later.** Relate the name to some gimmick that will help you remember it. Here are some associations that work:
    - A celebrity or friend with the same name
    - The business where the person works
    - A rhyme or pun
    - Something about the person's appearance that associates with his or her name

Most of all, tell yourself you *will* remember the name. You'd be surprised how effective it is just to place names in your recall memory consciously. Many of us say, "Oh, I can *never* remember names!"—and sure enough, we don't!

DO YOU KNOW YOUR CUSTOMER'S NAMES?

What customers do you regularly call by name? ______________________________

Do you have opportunities to remember and use the names of other customers you do business with? ______________________________

How do you feel when people remember and use your name? ______________________________

Are there any possible problems that might arise if you use a customer's name? ______________________________

TIP 46

Offer to Do the Job

Have you ever had to deal with an agency or a company that kept transferring you to another department because you were not speaking to the right person? How did you feel being passed from person to person, each one cheerfully informing you that he or she couldn't help you?

In a TQM organization it is the job of every person to handle the business of the entire organization. Every person becomes responsible for delighting the customer, whatever it takes.

Although the customer has called the marketing department to report something that must be handled by the accounts payable department, do not punish the customer. He or she does not even need to know about his or her mistake. The appropriate way to handle such a situation is to thank the customer for calling, assure him or her that it will be taken care of as quickly as possible, and ask for his or her name and number and the details of the problem. Next, call the appropriate department and report the situation. Give all the information you have and ask when they will be able to solve it. If you find they cannot solve the problem, ask who can and call that department.

The customer should be spared your organization's internal mazes. Follow up with the department that agrees to handle the problem to see that it was corrected.

In short, take the responsibility for your entire organization to make sure your customers are glad that they do business with you.

TAKING RESPONSIBILITY CHECK-UP

Think back to your last customer (internal or external) contact. List two actions you could have taken, but didn't, that would have delighted your customer.

- ______________________________

  ____

- ______________________________

  ____

Reward Customers for Giving You Their Business

What can you do to "reward customers"?

Think of times that you were pleased with service you received:

- What was it that pleased you?
- Were the people simply prompt and courteous?
- Did they do something that pleasantly surprised you?
- Were you provided with additional goods or services beyond the norm?

Examples of simple "rewards":

- Answering the phone on the first or second ring
- Providing free coffee or other inexpensive refreshment
- Providing magazines or newspapers to waiting customers
- Giving a small gift to customers who bring service problems to your attention
- Giving a sincere smile and a handshake

Customers reward us with their business. We, in turn, reward them for doing business with us.

HOW DO YOU REWARD CUSTOMERS?

Brainstorm about "rewards" your department or organization could provide your customers:

What rewards would be appropriate for the *external* customers of your organization? ______________________________

____

____

What rewards would be appropriate for the *internal* customers in your organization? ______________________________

____

____

What rewards would *you* like to receive when you are the external or internal customer? ______________________________

____

____

TIP 48

Be Prompt in Straightening Out a Problem

Not all customer problems are your fault, but they *are* all problems. Customers need to know that you hear their concern and will do what is possible to correct the problem.

Time is of the essence when handling customer problems. A problem that is handled quickly will quickly cease to be a problem for the customer—and for you too! Sometimes it is hard to be motivated to handle customer problems immediately because you hope they will just "go away." Sadly, though, the reverse is true. The longer the problem is left alone, the more upset and insistent the customer will become.

A good rule of thumb is to "never let the sun set on a customer complaint" without taking action or seeking help.

PROMPT HANDLING OF CUSTOMER PROBLEMS QUICK-CHECK

What would it take to make sure that customer complaints are handled in your department within one day? ____________________

Could you implement such a system? ____________________

TIP 49

Make the Most of Your Telephone Contacts

A telephone call is often your only contact with an internal or external customer. Seize the opportunity to make the most of that contact. Your voice and attitude become the image of your organization or your department to the person on the other end of the line.

Always start your call with your name—both when you place a call and when you answer a call. By saying your name clearly and confidently, you avoid any awkward "Who are you?" questions. Even if you are calling on behalf of another person, say your name first and then follow it with the other person's name (i.e., "This is Lee Jones calling from the office of Dale Smith").

Use your voice to convey a feeling a helpfulness and confidence. Be pleasant and avoid sounding bored or overly stressed (even if you may feel that way!). Be prepared for calls you place by having the information you need in front of you.

Even though it may seem awkward, *make yourself smile* when you talk on the phone. Your smile will come through your voice.

With our rapidly expanding communications technology, there seems to be no end to new telephone services and equipment. Remember that the person you call may not be in the physical location of the number you dialed. Cellular phones and call forwarding can put that person just about anywhere in the world. Ask if it is a good time to talk (he or she may be holding on another line because your call came in via "call waiting"). Also, be courteous on answering machines and voice mail—they are here to stay. Clearly state your name, your organization and *your phone number* before you begin a message. If you give the vital information right at the beginning, your chances of being called back improve greatly.

TELEPHONE CONTACTS CHECK

Do you have any "telephone customers" that know you only via the phone? ____________________

____

____

How could you improve your telephone image or skills? ____________________

____

____

TIP 50

Keep Your Promises

Reliability is one of the foundations of trust—and trust is essential to quality. Trust means that customers will agree to pay a little more to know that your product or service will live up to their expectations.

Reliability is simply doing what you say you will do. It may seem easier just to tell people what you know they want to hear, but in the long run they will know what you did. Everyone has been to a restaurant that promised a table would be ready "in about five minutes" and then waited over half an hour. It doesn't make you any less hungry to be lied to; in fact, you usually end up hungry and *angry.*

The rule in a TQM organization is to tell your customers (both external and internal) the truth. Keep the promises that you make, and only make promises that you can keep. If you must promise something that you cannot completely control, such as when a shipment that has been lost in transit might be delivered, follow the axiom "under-promise—over-deliver."

A sign in a telephone service center says:

"You can't promise your customers sunny weather, but you can promise to hold an umbrella over them when it rains."

DO YOU KEEP YOUR WORD?

Are there times when you *must* make promises to either external or internal customers? ____________________

How can you make sure that you keep your promises? ____________________

What do you say or do if the realistic promise is not good enough and the customer wants an unrealistic assurance? ____________________

CASE STUDIES

Putting TQM into Practice

Case Studies

The case studies on the following pages illustrate a few of the ways that TQM concepts applied to the everyday work of an organization. Some of the case studies illustrate a point, some show how to deal with a problem.

The value of case studies is to give you a message and an example of how to approach problems that you may encounter in your own work environment. Use the case studies to begin a discussion. See if others on your team can "out-smart" the case study. Do you know a better way? Good, try it out.

The culture of any organization (family, nation, team or work group) is based on case studies, or stories, that illustrate a point, teach the organization's values and empower people to *think* and solve problems. Take some time in your team meeting to discuss your own "case studies." What has happened in your work life lately that merits being shared with others? Probably more than you think.

Consider making it an "assignment" for one team member to bring a case study of TQM in action to each team meeting. Rotate from member to member each week and give that person time to tell of an incident that shows how one or more of the three major themes of TQM were used to solve a problem or handle a situation:

- Focus on the Customer
- Involve the Entire Work Force in Decision Making
- Commit to Continuous Improvement

CASE STUDY #1
Creative Dissatisfaction in Action

Recognizing a Problem Is the First Step Toward Solving It

To emphasize the need for recognizing problems as opportunities, one small company with 50 employees decided to hold an open "competition" to find the most costly problem that had occurred in the company during the previous quarter.

Dozens of employees owned up to mistakes and snafus that had cost the company anywhere from a few dollars to a thousand dollars. All acknowledged their part in the error and presented their ideas for making changes to correct the problems or to make sure that they didn't recur.

When the company president described the error he had made that had cost the company tens of thousands of dollars, the room became very quiet. It was certainly the most costly mistake the company had made that quarter, or perhaps even that year. Imagine everyone's amazement as the president calmly presented the problem and his role in it and offered his suggestions for improvement.

It is important for *all levels* of an organization to be willing to seek out problems and work toward improvement. By being willing to present problems openly without blame or retribution, an organization can use creative dissatisfaction as an avenue toward zero defects.

CASE STUDY #2
Honoring Commitments

Why Are Some People Always Late?

At a seminar where participants had agreed to be in their seats within one minute after every break, there was a man who was *always* at least two or three minutes late. Everyone else would be in their seats, the presenter would begin the session, and then this man would burst through the back doors and hurry to his seat, whispering apologies to the people who were moving aside to allow him to get there.

After the first break on the second day, this same man came back over four minutes late. He smilingly hurried up the aisle toward his seat. He whispered to those who had to move aside for him that he had had a very important call to make—it took longer than he thought it would, and so on. He moved down the row and when he got to his seat he realized that there was someone sitting in his seat. He told the person sitting there that he was in the wrong seat—this was his assigned seat. The person refused to budge. The latecomer got the attention of the presenter and apologized for being late and then asked him to please tell this "intruder" to move.

"Oh, but he is not an intruder," the presenter told him. "That person is your *replacement*. While you were gone everyone voted to have him take your place so that we could get started on time. I'm sorry, but you don't have a seat anymore."

The man was furious, but silent. He looked around at the people in the seminar who smiled apologetically back at him as he had done to them so many times before.

Remember this the next time you are late or you "forget" to do something you have said you will do: If you don't care enough to honor your commitments to those who depend on you, the depth of their commitment and loyalty to you will be very shallow.

CASE STUDY #3

"The Second Right Answer" Offers a Second Chance

Sometimes Your First Idea Isn't Always Your Best Idea

When two companies merged as the result of a buyout, the employees knew that layoffs were certain. After all, they didn't need two personnel departments, two data entry departments, and so on.

The new company told the employees that it would take suggestions for their continued employment if they could make a financially sound case for their jobs. The employees of the data entry department met and discussed possible options. The first option was to provide an "out-sourcing" service to other companies that used data entry. This solution seemed to have all of the elements that the new management had requested: The employees would not cost the company money, yet they would continue to provide the services needed. Many data entry employees felt ready to take their idea to management as soon as possible. After all, they were facing a possible layoff deadline and they wanted to know where they stood.

A small group, however, felt the need to look for "the second right answer" before taking their idea to management. The second alternative was to distribute the data entry clerks to each of the departments they served. That would mean the end of the data entry department as a separate entity, but it would mean that the employees would stay within the company and do data entry and additional clerical tasks assigned by the manager of each department.

When the first idea was scuttled because the new management did not want the responsibility of recruiting "out-source" customers and dealing with billing and other customer-service tasks, the employees brought out their "second right answer." Assigning the employees to the departments that required data entry work and then broadening their job descriptions to include other clerical tasks benefited everyone. The departments received experienced employees that knew how to do the crucial data entry tasks, and the employees received additional training and job skills that made their jobs more enjoyable and valuable to the company.

CASE STUDY #4

Train Someone in Something You Do Well

Peer Training Offers Advantages to Both the Trainer and the Trainee

A high tech company that hires hearing-disabled workers was concerned about the isolation of the hearing-disabled employees from the rest of the work force. All of the nonhearing employees could use sign language, and they communicated well among themselves, but it was difficult for the hearing and the nonhearing employees to communicate with each other.

The first effort to remedy the situation was to bring in a professional sign language teacher to teach the hearing employees to sign. The employees were released from duties to attend sign classes, but the training did not significantly improve the communication gap because: the professional sign language teacher did not know the signs for the jargon or terminology used in this high tech work environment, and when the hearing-disabled employees tried to sign a conversation with the hearing workers, they were frustrated by the hearing workers' awkward early attempts to understand and to sign back.

After weeks of accepting that things were probably never going to change, one of the hearing-disabled workers made a suggestion to the others that nonhearing workers take the responsibility to teach their co-workers to sign. That would not only allow them to get to know their co-workers in a more relaxed, team-spirited environment, but it would also allow them to know their co-workers' level of expertise in sign language so they could communicate within that level. The third benefit was that the nonhearing employees knew the signs for technical words and concepts used in their unique work.

The response to the new sign language classes was enthusiastic, and now both hearing and nonhearing workers have achieved a higher level of self-esteem and expertise—not to mention the camaraderie and team spirit gained by having everyone "speak the same language."

CASE STUDY #5
Accepting the Challenge of Change

Empowerment Is a Natural Result of Taking the Responsibility That Comes with Change

In most traditional school districts the school budgets are created by the principals and the teachers simply make requests and hope they get the supplies they need. One innovative district decided, however, that the best way to make sure that teachers' needs were met was to make the teachers completely responsible for the entire curriculum budget, the part of the budget that deals with teaching the students.

At first some of the teachers were not in favor of the change. After all, how to budget was not part of their professional training. What if they made a mistake and ran out of a critical resource halfway through the year?

The majority of the teachers *were* in favor of being responsible for the budget, however. They had been unhappy with the powerless position of having to beg and plead for needed supplies, and they felt that they were in a better position to know what was truly critical since they were closer to the "customer"—the students.

The first year, the teachers took a long time to reach a consensus. Many resisted adding yet another task to their already hectic schedules. And some were afraid to give their approval to *any* budget because they were wary of the possible repercussions if they were wrong.

And there were a few glitches in that first year's budget. For instance, how did they ever approve a budget item of over $100 for royal purple construction paper? But all in all, the year went smoothly, and the teachers learned firsthand how difficult it is to predict what will be needed and when.

By the third year, the teachers were eager to tackle the budget. They felt confident in their choices, and they introduced new ideas for saving money so they could fund some new materials and teaching strategies.

The great thing about accepting change is that it empowers you to move on to even greater changes.

CASE STUDY #6

A Story from Your Organization

What was the situation?

Who was involved?

How was it handled or resolved?

What was the lesson learned or the TQM concept used?

Follow-Up

We are not at all skeptical about TQM. We believe in it, we practice it, we know it works. It isn't terribly complex or ridiculously simple; nor is it "voodoo management." It is mostly common sense, which translates into keeping your eye (and your ear) on your customer.

It makes good sense from a financial and business point of view to do what it takes to win customers and increase your market share. But we believe it makes good sense from a *personal* perspective as well. Let's face it, it is less stressful and more rewarding to work with people who treat each other with respect and consideration. And continuous improvement means you never get stuck in the rut of turning out the same old product or service for so many weeks (or months or years) that you just don't care about it anymore.

We would like to hear from you about your experiences in making TQM work for your organization. We enjoy "real life" stories and unique ideas. If you would like to share a story or an idea, or if you have a question that we might be able to help with, please write to us:

JoAnn Haberer & MaryLou Wendel Webb
P.O. Box 5782
Vancouver, WA 98668-5782

Recommended Reading List

Building a Total Quality Culture. Joe Batten. Crisp Publications, Menlo Park, CA, 1993.

Building Productive Teams. Glenn H. Varney. Jossey-Bass, San Francisco, CA, 1991.

Close to the Customer. James H. Donnelly, Jr. Business One Irwin, Homewood, IL, 1993.

Coaching for Commitment. Denis C. Kinlaw. University Associates, Inc., San Diego, CA, 1989.

Commit to Quality. Patrick L. Townsend. John Wiley & Sons, New York, 1990.

Confessions of Empowering Organizations. Ray Redburn et al. Association for Quality and Participation, Cincinnati, OH, 1991.

Delivering Knock Your Socks Off Service. Ron Zemke and Kristin Anderson. American Management Association, New York, 1991.

The Empowered Manager. "Positive Political Skills at Work." Peter S. Block. Jossey-Bass, San Francisco, CA, 1987.

Empowerment: A Practical Guide for Success. Cynthia D. Scott and Dennis T. Jaffe. Crisp Publications, Menlo Park, CA, 1991.

Firing On All Cylinders. Jim Clemmer. Business One Irwin, Homewood, IL, 1992.

How to Win Customers and Keep Them for Life. Michael LeBoeuf, Berkley Books, New York, 1987.

The Human Side of Enterprise. Douglas McGregor. McGraw-Hill, New York, 1985.

In Search of Excellence. Thomas Peters and Robert Waterman, Jr. Harper & Row, New York, 1982.

The Leadership Challenge. James M. Kouzes and Barry Z. Posner. Jossey-Bass, San Francisco, CA, 1988.

Leadership Is an Art. Max Dupree. Dell Publishing, 1989.

Management Practices: U.S. Companies Improve Performance Through Quality Efforts. United States General Accounting Office. GAO/NSIAD 91-190, Washington, DC, May 1991.

Managing Quality Through Teams. "A Workbook for Team Leaders and Members." Lawrence M. Miller and Jennifer Howard. Miller Consulting Group. Atlanta, GA, 1991.

The One Minute Manager. Kenneth Blanchard and Spencer Johnson. Berkeley Books, Berkeley, CA, 1981.

Out of the Crisis. W. Edwards Deming. MIT, Center for Advanced Engineering Study, Cambridge, MA, 1986.

The Power Pyramid: 10 Steps to Empowerment. Diane Tracy. William Morrow & Co., New York, 1990.

Principle-Centered Leadership. Stephen R. Covey. Summit Books, New York, 1990.

Quality in America. V. Daniel Hunt. Business One Irwin, Homewood, IL, 1992.

Quality Is Free. Philip Crosby. McGraw-Hill, New York, 1979.

Quality OR ELSE. Lloyd Dobyns and Clare Crawford-Mason. Houghton Mifflin, Boston, MA, 1991.

Quick and Easy Tips You Can Use to Keep Your Customers. Communications Briefings, 700 Black Horse Pike, Blackwood, NJ, 08012, 1990.

Reinventing Government. "How the Entrepreneurial Spirit Is Transforming the Public Sector." David Osborne and Ted Gaebler. Addison-Wesley Publishing, Reading, MA, 1992.

Self-Managing Teams. Robert Hicks and Diane Bone. Crisp Publications, Menlo Park, CA, 1992.

Service America. "Doing Business in the New Economy." Karl Albrecht and Ron Zemke. Publisher's Quality Press, 1985.

The Seven Habits of Highly Effective People. Stephen R. Covey. Summit Books, New York, 1990.

Team Building: An Exercise in Leadership. Revised Edition, Robert B. Maddux. Crisp Publications, Menlo Park, CA, 1992.

The Team Handbook. Peter R. Scholtes. Joiner Associates, Inc., 1988.

A Whack on the Side of the Head. Roger von Oech. Warner Books, New York, 1990.

Zapp!: Employee Empowerment. William C. Byham. Harmony Books, DDI, Pittsburgh, PA, 1990.

NOTES

NOTES

NOTES

We hope you enjoyed this book. If so, we have good news for you. This title is part of the best-selling ***FIFTY-MINUTE***™ ***Series*** of books. All ***Series*** books are similar in size and identical in price. Several are supported with training videos (identified by the symbol Ⓥ next to the title).

FIFTY-MINUTE Books and Videos are available from your distributor. A free catalog is available upon request from Crisp Publications, Inc., 1200 Hamilton Court, Menlo Park, California 94025.

FIFTY-MINUTE Series Books & Videos organized by general subject area.

Management Training:

Ⓥ	Coaching & Counseling	68-8
	Conducting Training Sessions	193-7
	Delegating for Results	008-6
	Developing Instructional Design	076-0
Ⓥ	Effective Meeting Skills	33-5
Ⓥ	Empowerment	096-5
	Ethics in Business	69-6
	Goals & Goal Setting	183-X
	Handling the Difficult Employee	179-1
Ⓥ	An Honest Day's Work: Motivating Employees	39-4
Ⓥ	Increasing Employee Productivity	10-8
Ⓥ	Leadership Skills for Women	62-9
	Learning to Lead	43-4
Ⓥ	Managing Disagreement Constructively	41-6
Ⓥ	Managing for Commitment	099-X
	Managing the Older Work Force	182-1
Ⓥ	Managing Organizational Change	80-7
	Managing the Technical Employee	177-5
	Mentoring	123-6
Ⓥ	The New Supervisor—Revised	120-1
	Personal Performance Contracts—Revised	12-2
Ⓥ	Project Management	75-0
Ⓥ	Quality at Work: A Personal Guide to Professional Standards	72-6
	Rate Your Skills As a Manager	101-5
	Recruiting Volunteers: A Guide for Nonprofits	141-4
	Risk Taking	076-9
	Selecting & Working with Consultants	87-4
	Self-Managing Teams	00-0
	Successful Negotiation—Revised	09-2
	Systematic Problem Solving & Decision Making	63-7

Management Training (continued):

Personal Improvement:

Human Resources & Wellness:

Human Resources & Wellness (continued):

	Productivity at the Workstation: Wellness & Fitness at Your Desk	41-8
	Professional Excellence for Secretaries	52-1
	Quality Interviewing—Revised	13-0
	Sexual Harassment in the Workplace	153-8
	Stress That Motivates: Self-Talk Secrets for Success	150-3
	Wellness in the Workplace	20-5
	Winning at Human Relations	86-6
	Writing a Human Resources Manual	70-X
V	Your First Thirty Days in a New Job	003-5

Communications & Creativity:

	The Art of Communicating	45-9
V	Writing Business Proposals & Reports—Revised	25-4
V	The Business of Listening	34-3
	Business Report Writing	122-8
	Creative Decision Making	098-1
V	Creativity in Business	67-X
	Dealing Effectively with the Media	116-3
V	Effective Presentation Skills	24-6
	Facilitation Skills	199-6
	Fifty One-Minute Tips to Better Communication	071-X
	Formatting Letters & Memos on the Microcomputer	130-9
	Influencing Others	84-X
V	Making Humor Work	61-0
	Speedreading in Business	78-5
	Technical Presentation Skills	55-6
	Technical Writing in the Corporate World	004-3
	Think on Your Feet	117-1
	Visual Aids in Business	77-7
	Writing Fitness	35-1

Customer Service/Sales Training:

	Beyond Customer Service: The Art of Customer Retention	115-5
V	Calming Upset Customers	65-3
V	Customer Satisfaction—Revised	084-1
	Effective Sales Management	31-0
	Exhibiting at Tradeshows	137-6
	Improving Your Company Image	136-8
	Managing Quality Customer Service	83-1
	Measuring Customer Satisfaction	178-3
	Professional Selling	42-4
V	Quality Customer Service—Revised	95-5
	Restaurant Server's Guide—Revised	08-4
	Sales Training Basics—Revised	119-8
	Telemarketing Basics	60-2
V	Telephone Courtesy & Customer Service—Revised	064-7

Small Business & Financial Planning:

The Accounting Cycle	146-5
The Basics of Budgeting	134-1
Consulting for Success	006-X
Creative Fund Raising	181-3
Credits & Collections	080-9
Direct Mail Magic	075-2
Financial Analysis: Beyond the Basics	132-5
Financial Planning with Employee Benefits	90-4
Marketing Your Consulting or Professional Services	40-8
Personal Financial Fitness—Revised	89-0
Publicity Power	82-3
Starting Your New Business—Revised	144-9
Understanding Financial Statements	22-1
Writing & Implementing a Marketing Plan	083-3

Adult Literacy & Learning:

Adult Learning Skills	175-9
Basic Business Math	24-8
Becoming an Effective Tutor	28-0
Building Blocks of Business Writing	095-7
Clear Writing	094-9
The College Experience: Your First Thirty Days on Campus	07-8
Easy English	198-8
Going Back to School: An Adult Perspective	142-2
Introduction to Microcomputers: The Least You Should Know	087-6
Language, Customs & Protocol for Foreign Students	097-3
Improve Your Reading	086-8
Returning to Learning: Getting Your G.E.D.	02-7
Study Skills Strategies—Revised	05-X
Vocabulary Improvement	124-4

Career/Retirement & Life Planning:

Career Discovery—Revised	07-6
Developing Strategic Resumes	129-5
Effective Networking	30-2
I Got the Job!—Revised	121-X
Job Search That Works	105-8
Plan B: Protecting Your Career from Change	48-3
Preparing for Your Interview	33-7